I Love You, Stinky Face

Written by Lisa McCourt

Illustrated by Cyd Moore

Cartwheel BOOKS®

SCHOLASTIC INC.

New York Toronto London Auckland Sydney
Mexico City New Delhi Hong Kong Buenos Aires

For Aimee ～ L. M.
For my most wonderful ones,
Lindsay and Branden ～ C. M.

ISBN 0-439-63469-5

Text copyright © 1997 by Lisa McCourt.
Illustrations copyright © 1997 by Cyd Moore.
All rights reserved. Published by Scholastic Inc.
SCHOLASTIC, CARTWHEEL BOOKS, and associated logos
are trademarks and/or registered trademarks of Scholastic Inc.

First published in hardcover by BridgeWater Books.
Produced by Boingo Books, Inc.

20 19 18 17 16 15 14   08

Printed in the U.S.A.   08

First Scholastic printing, October 2003

"I love you, my wonderful child," said Mama as she tucked me in.
But I had a question.

Mama, what if I were a **big, scary**

ape? Would you still love me then?

"If you were a big, scary ape, I would comb your whole hairy self to make sure you didn't have any tangles.

"And I would make your birthday cake out of bananas, and I would tell you, 'I love you, my big, scary ape.'"

But, Mama, but, Mama, what if I were a super smelly skunk, and I smelled so bad that my name was Stinky Face?

"Then I would give you a bath and sprinkle you with sweet-smelling powder.

"And if you still smelled bad, I wouldn't mind, and I would hug you tight and whisper in your ear, 'I love you, Stinky Face.'"

But, Mama, but, Mama, what if I were an alligator with big, sharp teeth that could bite your head off?

"Then I would buy you a bigger toothbrush for your big teeth and make sure that you brushed them every night so they'd stay healthy and strong.

"And if you had a sore throat, I would stick my head right inside your enormous jaws to make sure you were okay, and I would say, 'I love you, my ferocious alligator.'"

But, Mama, what if I were a terrible meat-eating dinosaur with razor-sharp claws that ripped my sheets to shreds every night while I slept?

"Then I would give you plenty of meat to eat, if that is what you liked. And I would sew your sheets back together every day, because, after all, ripping them would be an accident.

"And I would tuck you into your newly mended sheets every night and say, 'I love you, my sweet, terrible dinosaur.'"

"But, Mama, but, Mama, what if I were a swamp creature with slimy, smelly seaweed hanging from my body, and I couldn't ever leave the swamp or I would die?"

"Then I would build a house right next to the swamp, and I would stay with you and take care of you always. And when you splashed to the surface, I would say, 'I love you, my slimy little swamp monster.'"

But, Mama, but, Mama, what if I were a **Green Alien** from Mars, and I ate bugs instead of peanut butter?

"Then I would dress
you in colors that
showed off your
nice green skin . . .

and I would pack
your lunch box with
beetles and spiders
and ants and
grasshoppers and
the tastiest bugs
you ever had.
And I would pack
a note with all the
bugs that said,
'I love you,
little greenie.
Bon appétit.'"

But, Mama, but, Mama, what if I were a **Cyclops**, and I had just one big, gigantic eye in the middle of my head?

"Then I would look right into your gigantic eye and say, 'I love you, my little cyclops,' and I would sing you a lullaby until your one gigantic eyelid got droopier and droopier, and it finally closed and you fell fast asleep."

I love you, Mama.

"And I love you, my wonderful child."